Minute Help Guides Presents:

A Newbies Guide to Excel 2013 RT

Minute Help Guides

Minute Help Press

<u>www.minutehelp.com</u>

Cover Image © Kenishirotie - Fotolia.com

Table of Contents

Introduction

In the 22-odd years since the company unveiled their suite of productivity programs, Microsoft Office has become synonymous with *serious* computer work. Whether it's a Fortune 500 conglomerate's all-important spreadsheet or a homemaker's recipe catalog, MS Office has been the dominant force in productivity applications for a very long time. While Apple, Google and their ilk have certainly created a competitive atmosphere in recent years, nobody can touch the usability, customization, or sheer power of the Microsoft Office suite.

Now, with the release of their first official tablet computer, Microsoft has upped the ante, optimizing and customizing Office for the touch screen powerhouse they've dubbed Windows RT. While a good chunk of the functionality that Office users have gotten used to over the years remains the same, there are a few new things to get acquainted with.

The Surface and other Windows RT tablets are especially well suited to working with Microsoft Excel. Having the ability to Crunch numbers while on the go is only going to become more and more important in the modern business landscape. In short, Excel RT is a *godsend* for productivity.

While almost anyone can find their way around a Word document with a couple of minutes of practice, a lot of people are intimidated by the sheer power of Excel.

This guide will take you through the basics of Microsoft Excel, the most widely used spreadsheet program on the planet. We'll show you what you need to get started, everything from creating simple worksheets and saving your documents (with SkyDrive!) to turning your finished spreadsheets into powerful (and beautiful) visualizations of your data. Whether you've been using spreadsheet applications for years, or you're still clinging to your old adding machine and ledger system, we'll not only show you how to craft perfect Excel documents, we'll have fun doing it!

At a glance, Excel RT 2013 looks like an incredibly complex program. It *can* be, but it definitely doesn't *have* to be. This guide will teach you what you need to know to get to work *right now*, leaving the fluff and the head scratching for people with time to waste.

Ready to get started? Let's go!

Part One: Getting Started with Excel 2013 RT

First Things First: Supported Devices, Keyboard Covers, and Other Accessories

Before we dive right in, there are a couple of things we'll need to discuss to make sure you're able to get the most out of Office RT. While this guide is primarily geared toward Surface RT users, Microsoft has licensed the software to a few other hardware companies, which means that you *could* be using any one of these other devices:

- Asus VivoTab RT
- Dell XPS 10
- Samsung Ativ
- Lenovo IdeaPad Yoga (RT)

Office RT will function identically on these other devices, but this section will focus on peripherals you'll want to have for the Surface.

> *Note: Microsoft has released two different versions of the Surface tablet, one labeled Surface RT and one labeled Surface Pro. Since the Surface Pro is essentially a full-fledged computer shoved into a tablet form factor, they do not include any version of Office with it. Office RT is, in fact, a specially coded version of the software meant to be used with what's called ARM processors – chips used primarily in mobile devices. The Surface Pro uses standard X86 chips, which makes it 100% incompatible with Office RT. Long story short: if you bought a Surface Pro, you'll have to buy your own copy of Excel, which will have a slightly different set of features than the version discussed in this guide.*

Covers

While the Surface RT doesn't automatically ship with a keyboard, Microsoft has engineered two different, equally elegant solutions: the 'touch' cover and the 'type' cover:

The touch cover is not really a keyboard, at least not exactly. It's an incredibly thin, touch-sensitive mat, with a keyboard layout. Completely flat to the touch, typing on it can take a little getting used to. The type cover is more akin to a regular keyboard – the keys have a fair bit of 'travel', which means they move when you press down.

Either solution is perfectly suitable, depending on your preferences, but we highly recommend picking one up. An on-screen keyboard is fine for web browsing or jotting down small notes, but you're definitely going to need a real keyboard to get anything bigger accomplished. Both of these keyboard covers are available for around $120 – the rest of this guide will assume that you've got one.

Both of these keyboard covers also come with a built-in trackpad, which functions in the same way that a laptop trackpad does. For those of you that dislike trackpads, we also recommend picking up a USB mouse. Hundreds of them are compatible with the Surface RT, but if compatibility isn't specifically listed on the model you'd like to pick up, check out www.microsoft.com/compatibility to be sure. A whole lot of devices are compatible, even ones you'd *never* think would be. Case in point: Apple's Magic Multi-Touch Trackpad works flawlessly, according to the compatibility check:

Apple Magic Multi-Touch Trackpad

MC380LL/A

Available for:

Windows 8	Windows RT	Windows 7

Compatibility status may vary by operatin

Apple

Homepage   Support   Contact

The Magic Trackpad is the first
multi-touch trackpad designed to
work with your Mac desktop ...

Show more...

Model	Status
MC380LL/A	✓ Compatible No Action Required

Community ratin

Compatible : **3** Votes
Not compatible : **0** Votes

Give us your vot·

| Compatible | Not comp |

One important thing to consider: Excel, as you've no doubt realized, is primarily a numbers application. Portable keyboards are, by their very nature, Ill-suited to working with numbers, owing to their lack of a dedicated number pad. Not to worry: there are quite a few USB-powered number pads available for a lot less money than you'd think.

These dedicated number pads will really make your life easier if you plan to spend a lot of time entering data using your Windows RT tablet.

*Just like with the USB mice we discussed earlier, head to www.microsoft.com/compatibility to double check that the number pad you're considering purchasing is compatible.

Crunching the Numbers: A Quick Excel Primer

If you're already familiar with Excel and/or the concept of a spreadsheet program, feel free to skip this section of the guide. There's still plenty to learn, but this section will take a look at what *exactly* Excel RT is, who it's for, and what the program can do for you.

In prehistoric times (the beginning of history until the late 1970s, for our purposes), if you needed to do some complex calculations, this was among the most solid of options:

If you wanted to, say, create an expense report for your thriving abacus business, you bought a ledger, a pencil, and a $7,000 portable calculator.

Once you got fed up with that, you'd just hire an accountant and be done with it. The largest companies would sometimes purchase a single refrigerator-sized computer (for $50,000 at a minimum) to help with the arithmetic, but the average person couldn't even fathom *owning* a computer, let alone teaching themselves how to use it. Things went on that way until the late 1970s. When Apple, IBM, and all of the other early personal computer companies started seriously thinking about what consumers might actually want from these new machines. Enter: VisiCalc and Lotus 1-2-3.

These two early spreadsheet programs did more to help the adoption of computers in the home than almost anything else. In fact, researchers and scholars now refer to the electronic spreadsheet as the very first "killer app", the first time anything computer-related turned from a *want* into a *need* for the average consumer. Excel came along with some improvements and stole the limelight from competing spreadsheet programs sometime in the mid-90s, and – as they say – the rest is history. Nowadays, when we talk about spreadsheets, we're talking about Excel.

So what exactly *is* this mysterious-sounding program?

In the simplest of terms, Excel is an electronic spreadsheet program. It's designed to help you organize, store, and manipulate all kinds of data. This can be anything from sports statistics, a catalog of a store's comic books, your family's budget, or a Fortune 500 company's profit projections. Excel exists to do the heavy lifting for you, but, as with anything this powerful, you'll have to set it up to do what you want it to do. That's where this guide comes in.

While Excel RT 2013 is perfectly suited to complex business type stuff, this guide will mostly focus on the sorts of things that the average user would want to know. We can do some pretty cool stuff with Excel, things that you might not think about are made possible with Excel RT, and we'll go over a lot of them. Here's a small sampling of the things we can create with Excel:

- **Schedules**
- **Address Books**
- **Personal Inventories**
- **Monthly Budgets**

Once you've created a spreadsheet using Excel RT 2013, the fun really begins. Over the course of this guide we'll show you how to take all of that newly organized data and turn it into something beautiful. Like all the other Office RT programs, we'll be able to dress up our documents with SmartArt, charts, graphs, and all the colors of the rainbow, turning something that looks like this:

	A	B	C	D	
1	Region	1990_total	1990_urban	1990_rural	1
2	UNITED STATES	248,709,873	187,053,487	61,656,386	
3	Northeast Region	50,809,229	40,091,737	10,717,492	
4	New England Division	13,206,943	9,829,175	3,377,768	
5	Maine	1,227,928	547,824	680,104	
6	New Hampshire	1,109,252	565,670	543,582	
7	Vermont	562,758	181,149	381,609	
8	Massachusetts	6,016,425	5,069,603	946,822	
9	Rhode Island	1,003,464	863,381	140,083	
10	Connecticut	3,287,116	2,601,548	685,568	
11	Middle Atlantic Division	37,602,286	30,262,562	7,339,724	
12	New York	17,990,455	15,164,047	2,826,408	
13	New Jersey	7,730,188	6,910,220	819,968	
14	Pennsylvania	11,881,643	8,188,295	3,693,348	
15	Midwest Region	59,668,632	42,774,196	16,894,436	
16	East North Central Division	42,008,942	31,073,858	10,935,084	
17	Ohio	10,847,115	8,039,409	2,807,706	
18	Indiana	5,544,159	3,598,099	1,946,060	
19	Illinois	11,430,602	9,668,552	1,762,050	

Into something with a little more visual appeal:

The RT version of Excel is *slightly* more limited than its desktop counterpart. Macros, VBA (Visual Basic for Applications), and data modeling are omitted from this release, primarily for compatibility reasons. As such, we're not going to discuss any of these things over the course of this guide.

> *Microsoft has deemed these items not really all that important for the home user anyway, and we're inclined to agree with them. There's still plenty to learn without these overly complex features. In any case, if it turns out that you need these features, you'll have to spring for the full PC version of the software.*

But let's not get ahead of ourselves. In the next section, we'll go over all the steps necessary to update Office RT 2013 to its final version.

Updating/Finalizing Office RT

As you may have already noticed, Windows RT devices shipped with a 'preview' version of all the Office RT apps. Luckily, it's a snap to update it to the final version. According to Microsoft, this update should happen automatically, but that wasn't the case in our experience – we actually attempted an automatic update 3 times before we gave up. Have no fear though; just follow these simple steps to get yourself updated.

> *Note: For some reason, this update doesn't cancel out the original 'preview edition' completely. If you ever have to reset your RT device back to factory defaults, you'll have to go through this update process again. We're not sure why, but it's something you may have to deal with in the future.*

To get started with updating, just bring up the charms bar by swiping right to left. Once you've done that, tap the 'settings' charm:

Once you've done that, you'll be taken to the settings menu, which will look something like this:

To find the update menu, tap 'Change PC Settings'. This will bring up the more advanced menu, which will look like this:

Tap 'Windows Update' to continue. Once there, tap the button labeled 'Check for Updates'. After a few moments, you'll find a list of updates that Microsoft wants to apply. Go ahead and tap 'Install' and let it do its work. Depending on the number of updates that are found, this could take a little while. Trust us; it's worth the hassle to stay updated.

Once you've applied all the updates, your Office apps should no longer be labeled 'Preview' and should look like this on the Home Screen:

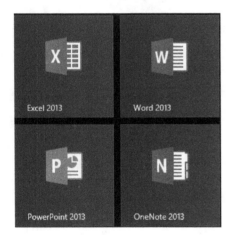

That's all there is to it. We're almost ready to dive right in, there's really only one more thing to set up: SkyDrive.

Your Documents in the Cloud: Setting up SkyDrive

Over the last few years, you've probably heard about "The Cloud" and its impact on computing. If you don't know any better, it sounds sort of scary and complicated. Rest assured that it's not. "The Cloud" is really just a buzzword – it's shorthand for online storage and nothing more. How does this relate to your Windows RT tablet?

If you're like most people, you probably have a few internet-connected devices lying around. You might use your desktop computer for some things, while other tasks are relegated to your smart phone or tablet. All these different gadgets are great for getting stuff done, except in one crucial way: how do you get your stuff from one device to another? How do you keep everything organized and up to date? Microsoft's answer to that is SkyDrive, and it's a great solution.

Microsoft has included 10 GB of SkyDrive cloud storage with every Surface tablet, while users of the other Windows tablets we discussed earlier will only have the 7 GB that comes for free. Users of cloud storage services like Dropbox or iCloud will be familiar with the concept behind Microsoft's SkyDrive, but the company's take on it is a little bit different, especially for Windows RT tablets.

Basically, SkyDrive is a folder (or group of folders) stored on the Internet, but accessible only to you and your devices. Copying a file from your computer to SkyDrive will make the file available instantaneously across all of your other SkyDrive-enabled devices. Setting up SkyDrive on your PC is crucial, especially if you use Office on devices other than your Windows RT tablet.

For example, let's say you've created a worksheet in Excel on your PC. You're sitting in the living room, watching television, when you suddenly remember a cell that you've forgotten to include. You can just pull the same file up on your Surface tablet and edit it without having to trudge back to your home office. The changes you make from the living room will automatically be applied to the file on your PC.

> *Since this guide will primarily focus on working with Excel RT, perhaps a better example would be creating a spreadsheet on your Surface tablet, and then saving it to SkyDrive for later use.*

To get started, we'll have to download the SkyDrive application to whichever devices you'd like. In Windows 8 or on your Windows RT tablet, that's as easy as searching for the app in the App Store and downloading it. If you're using another operating system, like OSX, Windows 7, or Windows Vista, it's a little bit more complicated.

To download the application, head over to www.microsoft.com. Once there, you'll notice a search bar in the upper right hand corner. Type 'SkyDrive' in the search bar and click search. The first result will be the SkyDrive app. Click again to download it.

Once it's downloaded, click to open the file and install it. Follow the prompts and enter your Microsoft ID and password in the fields. Make sure it's the same ID you use on your Windows RT device. That's all there is to it. You'll now have a folder on your desktop that looks like this:

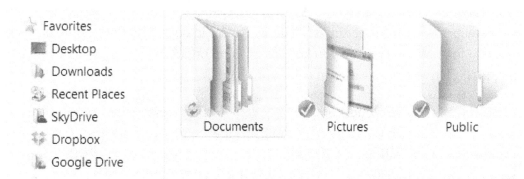

Copy whatever you'd like to it: documents, music, videos, etc. Whatever you copy will almost instantly appear within the SkyDrive app on your Windows RT tablet:

As a special bonus to users of Windows 8, installing SkyDrive will allow you to synchronize the settings of all of your Windows 8 and Windows RT devices. Your tile layout, background, system settings – all of it will match up perfectly if you want it to. Of course, you always have the ability to opt-out of that. For more info on Live Tiles and customization, consult "The Newbies Guide to the Microsoft Surface Tablet", available at www.minutehelpguides.com or from any major bookseller.

Now that you've set up the SkyDrive app, you can share the files on your Surface to it. It's as easy as swiping in the charms bar and tapping Share:

To make it even easier, Excel RT has a built-in SkyDrive solution. Simply tap to save the document you're working on and (after installing it on your Windows RT device) SkyDrive will appear as an option:

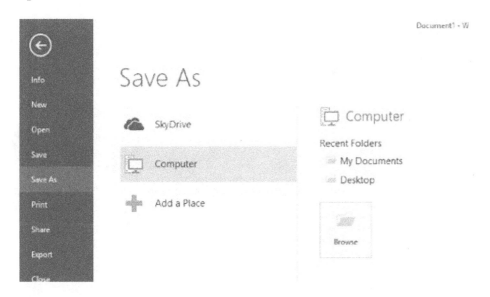

But, let's not get ahead of ourselves. In the next section, we'll begin to learn the basics and find our way around the program.

Ready? Let's go

Part Two: Using Excel 2013 RT

Navigating Excel 2013 RT – The Basics

In this section, we're going to discuss a few concepts that will help you understand the basics of the Excel RT program. The information is a little bit dense, so feel free to read it a couple of times to make sure you understand the material. We promise that everything will make perfect sense once you've used the program a few times.

Excel RT is broken down into a couple of different things (with a couple of different names). It can get confusing, so let's put it as simply as possible. Don't worry; we'll go over all of this stuff in detail a little later in this guide.

- **Workbook** – a 'workbook' is your spreadsheet file. By default, it will have the .xlsx extension. Inside a workbook, you can have several different spreadsheets, but they will all be contained within a single file.
- **Worksheet** – 'worksheets' are the individual spreadsheets that make up your workbook. By default, Excel RT 2013 places a single worksheet in any new workbook. You can use just that one or add more. A good example of this would be adding a new worksheet for every month of the year for your family's budget. Other versions of Microsoft Excel place 3 worksheets in each workbook by default.

Make sense? Good. Let's move on.

Each worksheet is made up of rows and columns. The rows are horizontal, while the columns are vertical. Rows are numbered, while columns are lettered. The points at which rows and columns intersect are known as cells. The cells are made up of boxes on the screen and are identified using the number and letter of the column and row where they are placed:

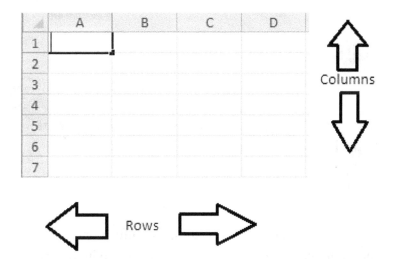

In the example above, the cell that's highlighted is cell A1. The labeling scheme goes on like that into (almost) infinity. You enter the information into the cells, changing them from the blank spaces they were into the bones of your spreadsheet. These cells can each contain one of several things:

- **Text** – cells can be (and often are) nothing but text, just like the words you're reading now. Plain text is used, generally speaking, to add a label to a row or a column.
- **Formulas** – think of formulas as if they're math problems. These formulas start with the equal sign (=) and are where all the calculations are done within the spreadsheet. For example, if we were to place the formula **=1+1** into cell A1, we'd end up with this:

	A	B	C
1	=1+1		
2			
3			
4			
5			
6			
7			

	A	B	C
1	2		
2			
3			
4			
5			
6			
7			

See how it did the math for us? Despite the potential complexity of the data you'll be entering, that's all a formula is, in essence.

- **Values** – values are numbers, times, dates, or logical answers (like true or false). We can enter any information we'd like to in a cell, and then refer to it, and manipulate the data using a formula. As an example, we entered 6 numbers, representing test scores for a student in a classroom. We entered the values starting at A2, and continuing until A7. At C8, we entered a formula to tell Excel to display the average of the test scores. Here's what came out:

	A	B	C	D
1	Sally's Test Scores			
2	95			
3	100			
4	85			
5	100			
6	95			
7	80			
8	Sally's Average:		92.5	
9				

As you can see, cells A1, B1, A8, and B8 are made up of text. A2, A3, A4, A5, A6, and A7 are values. C8 is also a value, but underneath the hood, it's actually a formula:

=AVERAGE(A2:A7)

Now, by default, all of the cells, rows, and columns are the same size. Everything is uniform, but sometimes the text you'd like to enter is a bit larger than the space provided. As you can see in the above example, the phrase "Sally's Test Scores" is actually almost twice the size of the A1 cell. With text, the words will automatically continue into the next row, provided the row next to it is blank. With numbers, however, it's not quite so easy.

If you're working with numbers larger than the default size of the cell, you won't be able to actually see the number. For example, we created this sample equation and placed it in cell A2:

```
=11*300000000
```

Now, the actual answer to that equation is 3,300,000,000. As you might've guessed, that number is far too large to fit in the cell, leaving us with this:

2	3.3E+09
3	
4	

While the number is still *in there*, and viewable from the formula bar (which we'll discuss momentarily), we can't exactly make use of 3.3E+09, can we? Luckily, it's super easy to change the size of the columns and rows. To do this, just find the column or row you'd like to resize and point your cursor (or finger) at the grey line on the right side of it at the top. Once you've done that, simple click and hold, then drag the row or column to resize it. You'll know that you've made it large enough when the 3.3E+09 notation (in our example) turns back into the number you'd like displayed:

A2

Width: 20.43 (148 pixels)

	A	B	C
1	2		
2	3300000000		
3			

*Changing the display size of columns and rows will also come in handy when it comes time to present your information in a more visual manner. Separating your information into visually appealing chunks makes a world of difference when it comes to the readability of your spreadsheets, which we'll go over in a later section of this guide.

Now that we've covered the basics, let's dig a little deeper and learn all about Excel RT 2013's menu system.

Ready? Let's go!

The Ribbon Menu and the Excel 2013 RT Interface

Now that we've talked a little bit about the fundamentals of an Excel spreadsheet, it's time to take a minute and go over all the parts that make up the Excel 2013 RT interface. It might look a little complex (or even intimidating) at first, but – trust us – it's a lot simpler than it looks. Starting from the top, here's a breakdown of everything that's above the actual spreadsheet:

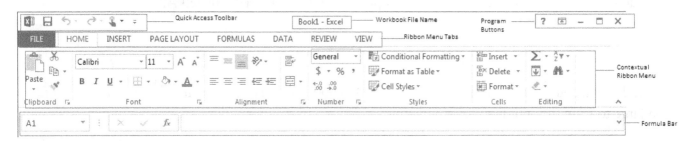

- **Quick Access Toolbar** – this area is a customizable little toolbar that holds several commonly used commands. By default, it'll contain (from left to right): *maximize/minimize, save, undo, redo, the touch/mouse optimization toggle,* and a dropdown list of other possible commands to display here.

  While 'save' and 'maximize/minimize' are pretty self-explanatory, the undo/redo functions and the touch/mouse toggle require a little explanation.

  Basically, anything you do within Excel RT 2013 can be undone. Anything from changing the size of a cell to entered text or formulas can be undone by tapping undo. This works one step at a time, back through the beginning of your document, generally speaking. Redo works the same way, but only in reverse after you've undone something.

  The touch/mouse optimization toggle is an interesting, if underused, command. Basically, when using any Office program on a touch-optimized device like the Surface RT, your fingers can sometimes get in the way when you're trying to do something with them. Tapping this toggle will enable you to change the layout of all the menu items to more closely match your input style. If you're using a mouse/keyboard to interact with Excel (which we recommend), keep the toggle on 'mouse'. If you'd rather use your fingers, select 'touch'. Here's what will happen:

Notice the difference? This is the exact same Ribbon menu from the illustration above, but optimized for touch. Everything's a little bigger, and a little easier to touch with your fingers.

- **Workbook File Name** – this area contains the name of the workbook that you're currently working in. By default, Excel labels workbooks that you haven't yet saved as "Book1", "Book2", etc. The number is based on the order in which you created a workbook. If you have three workbooks currently open (and unsaved), then the first one will be labeled "Book1". You can change the same of your file at any time by clicking (or tapping) "File" and then "Save As" and typing in whatever name you like.
- **Program Buttons** – to access certain program-wide functions, look here. You'll find a link to Excel's built-in help file, as well as options for closing the program and/or resizing the window that Excel is displayed in. Perhaps most importantly, there is also a toggle here to auto-hide the ribbon menu. If working on a smaller device like the Surface RT, it's sometimes helpful to do auto-hide, which will remove the ribbon menu until you hover over it.
- **Ribbon Menu Tabs** – As we'll discuss in a moment, this section is used to separate all of the various ribbon menus into cohesive, logical pieces. The 'File' tab is always shaded dark green and will take you to 'backstage view', while the currently in-use tab is highlighted in green.
- **Contextual Ribbon Menu** – this is the main menu system for Excel RT 2013. Depending on the tab you've chosen, the options displayed here will change. Most of your time will be spend in the 'home' tab, which contains most of the common menu items. We'll go over the ribbon in detail in a moment.
- **The Formula Bar** – everything you enter into a cell can also be entered in the formula bar. The formula bar will also display whatever is in the current active cell. It's often easier to enter things into the formula bar rather than into the cells themselves. It's especially useful when (like in our earlier example) the information entered into a cell is larger than the cell itself.

While everything has its purpose, nothing you see is more important than the ribbon menu. The ribbon menu is where we'll head to accomplish everything we'll be doing with this guide. We'll go over the details when the time comes, but for now, here's a general overview of what the ribbon menu contains:

- **File** – tapping here will bring you to what's known as the 'backstage view', which is where you'll save your files, open new or existing workbooks, print, and share your work.
- **Home** – this is where the majority of your time will be spent with the ribbon menu. Just like with other Office applications like Word or PowerPoint, Home contains the formatting options for text, all of the clipboard-type commands (cut, paste, etc.), and various other worksheet editing tools that we'll go over as we need them.
- **Insert** – like the name implies, we'll select this tab when we need to insert something into our worksheet – tables, charts, diagrams, clipart, SmartArt – this is where all of that stuff lives.
- **Page Layout** – this tab is where we'll go to change the overall look of our worksheets, mostly in preparation for printing or completion.
- **Formulas** – all of the more complex ways we'll interact with formulas are contained here. A lot of this stuff is beyond the scope of this guide, but we'll go over the basics when we get to them.

- **Data** – this area contains all of the complex data manipulation stuff like data validation and 'what if' analysis. Like Formulas, a lot of this stuff is strictly for the super-advanced business user, but we'll spend a few moments here a little later.
- **Review** – much like other Office programs, this area contains options for spellchecking, translations, commenting, and grammar checking. This is also where we'll go to protect our cells and worksheets from being edited once we've finished with them. More on that a little later.
- **View** – this area contains the options for changing the look of the cells within your spreadsheet. This is where we'll zoom and inspect different visual approaches for our workbooks.

While the ribbon menu is incredibly important, there is another way to access some important commands in Excel RT 2013. To bring up a context menu of commonly used commands, simply right click on an active cell. Once you've done that, you'll be greeted with a menu that looks something like this:

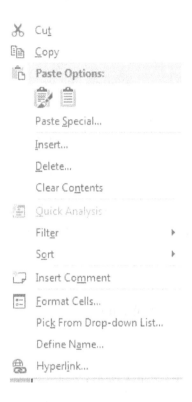

As you can see, cutting, copying, pasting, and cell formatting can all be accomplished from this menu, just like they can from the ribbon menu that we just discussed. Right clicking to bring up the context menu can save you a lot of time, once you get used to the commands that are available from there.

Speaking of time saving, now would be a good time to discuss one important new feature of Excel 2013 RT. It's called 'flash fill' and it'll make your life a whole lot easier. What is this magical flash fill? Let's take a second to explain it.

Let's say that we're going to create a spreadsheet with monthly sales figures for our business. We'll start with January 2012, so let's type January 2012 into our spreadsheet in cell A1:

A1 | fx | 1/1/2012

	A	B	C	D
1	Jan-12			
2				
3				
4				
5				
6				
7				
8				
9				
10				
11				
12				
13				

Once we've done that, you'll see that Excel automatically formats the date into a standardized format: Jan-12 in the cell, and the more accurate 1/1/2012 in the formula bar. So, if we want to enter in data for an entire year or more, we'd ordinarily have to continue typing the date into the other cells, i.e. February 2012 in A2, March 2012 in A3 and so on. With Flash Fill, that's no longer necessary. Excel 2013 will figure out what you want and allow you to automatically fill in the information. To do this, first find the small green square in the bottom right hand corner of cell A1, where you entered the date. This is called the fill button. Click it, and then drag it down for as many rows as you'd like. Once you've done that, you'll be presented with properly formatted monthly dates for as many rows as you want:

A1 | fx | 1/1/2012

	A	B	C
1	Jan-12		
2	Feb-12		
3	Mar-12		
4	Apr-12		
5	May-12		
6	Jun-12		
7	Jul-12		
8	Aug-12		
9	Sep-12		
10	Oct-12		
11	Nov-12		
12	Dec-12		
13	Jan-13		
14	Feb-13		
15	Mar-13		
16	Apr-13		
17	May-13		
18	Jun-13		
19	Jul-13		
20	Aug-13		
21	Sep-13		
22	Oct-13		
23	Nov-13		
24	Dec-13		
25	Jan-14		
26	Feb-14		
27	Mar-14		
28			
29			

Now, do you see the little box on the bottom right of the new data we just created? Click here if the data that was flash filled isn't exactly what you wanted. There will be a lot more options for the data you'd like auto-filled. More often than not, what you originally wanted will show up here:

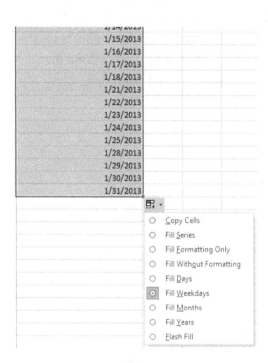

Pretty cool, huh? This works for a lot of different kinds of data, and will really come in handy when you begin creating spreadsheets of your own.

Now that we've learned a little more about Excel's interface, it's time to dive right in and begin creating our first spreadsheet.

Ready? Let's do it!

Creating Your First Worksheet

We've spent a little bit of time gaining a theoretical understanding of the Excel 2013 RT system, and now it's time to put that knowledge to use by creating a simple spreadsheet of our own. Feel free to follow along with us, substituting your own data if you wish. Open the Excel RT 2013 program by finding it either on your Start Screen or within the 'all apps' listing by swiping up on the charms bar. Once you've done that, you'll be presented with a screen that looks like this:

As you can see, there are quite a few options here. We'll come back to them a little later in this guide, but for now, just click (or tap) on 'Blank Workbook' to open a new blank Excel document. Once you've done that, you'll be presented with the (by now) familiar Excel spreadsheet screen:

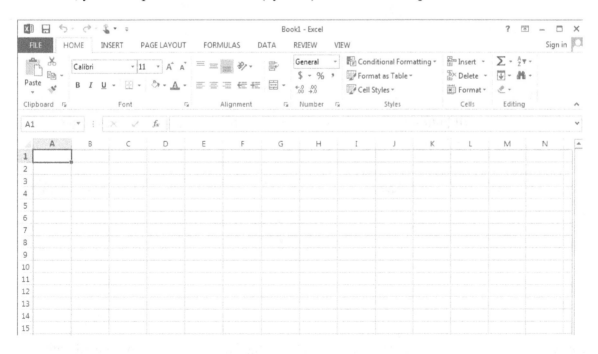

Let's create a simple expense report for a small business. The first thing we'll do is get all of our text in order. Click on cell A1 and type 'Monthly Expenses'. Once you've done that, hit enter, then hit enter again. The active cell will now be A3. Type 'Paper', then hit enter. Type each of the following words, hitting enter after each of them: Postage, Envelopes. Boxes, Misc., Total. Total should be in cell A8.

Once you've done that, click on cell B2. Type Jan and hit enter. Once you've done that, find the fill button in the lower right hand corner (that we discussed a little earlier) and click on it. From there, drag the cursor to the right until you've landed on M2. Cell M2 should be labeled Dec, while each cell before it in that row will be labeled with the previous month. You should have something that looks like this:

	A	B	C	D	E	F	G	H	I	J	K	L	M
1	Monthly Expenses												
2		Jan	Feb	Mar	Apr	May	Jun	Jul	Aug	Sep	Oct	Nov	Dec
3	Paper												
4	Postage												
5	Envelopes												
6	Boxes												
7	Misc												
8	Total												
9													
10													

Now we've got our basic outline. We'll be filling in dollar amounts in each cell, but first we've got to tell Excel what kind of data these cells are going to contain. To do this, we're going to activate the first cell that we'll be putting data into. In this case that's B3. Once you've done that, use the fill button to highlight the entire row from B2 to M2:

	A	B	C	D	E	F	G	H	I	J	K	L	M
1	Monthly Expenses												
2		Jan	Feb	Mar	Apr	May	Jun	Jul	Aug	Sep	Oct	Nov	Dec
3	Paper												
4	Postage												
5	Envelopes												
6	Boxes												
7	Misc												
8	Total												
9													

Once you've done that, use the fill button again to highlight M2-M8. Now every cell that we'll be entering numbers into will be highlighted:

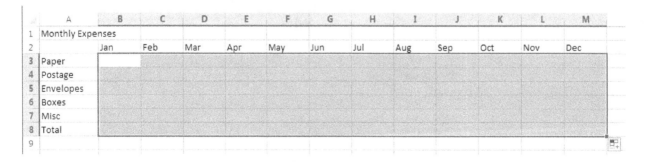

To format these cells, just right click anywhere within the highlighted area. You'll be presented with a context menu that looks like this:

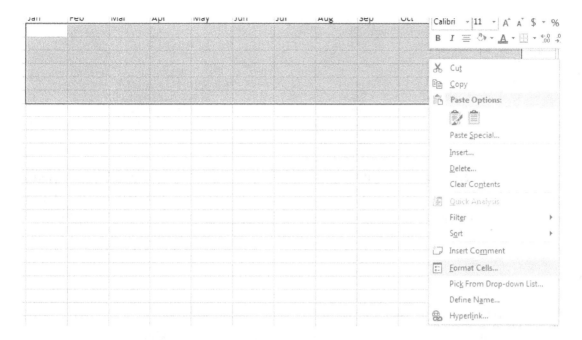

Find the menu item labeled 'Format Cells' and click there. You'll be presented with a pop-up window with a bunch of different formatting options:

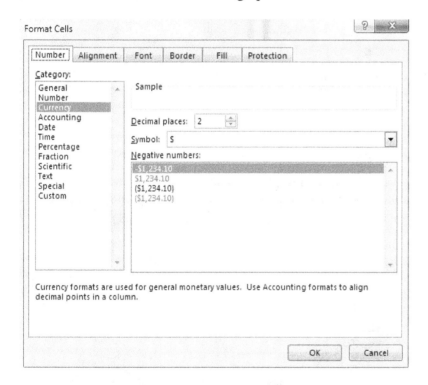

Click on 'Currency' and then click 'OK'. Now every number we enter will be converted into a dollar amount. Begin filling in the data, remembering to use a decimal place for cents. When you've finished entering data into a cell, you can hit enter to move down one row, or hit the right arrow to move right one column. Make sure to leave the 'Total' row blank. We'll be dealing with that in a moment.

Once you've filled in the data, your spreadsheet should look something like this:

	A	B	C	D	E	F	G	H	I	J	K	L	M
1	Monthly Expenses												
2		Jan	Feb	Mar	Apr	May	Jun	Jul	Aug	Sep	Oct	Nov	Dec
3	Paper	$11.00	$12.40	$14.78	$99.00	$0.00	$123.40	$33.00	$346.88	$0.00	$33.00	$35.00	$35.88
4	Postage	$14.32	$34.66	$666.00	$645.00	$44.00	$4,444.00	$45.55	$3,556.00	$12.00	$14.56	$333.88	$345.30
5	Envelopes	$12.33	$12.33	$34.00	$12.33	$12.33	$12.33	$12.33	$12.33	$12.33	$12.33	$12.33	$12.33
6	Boxes	$144.33	$12.33	$344.00	$44.00	$445.60	$66.66	$67.77	$565.33	$45.00	$555.40	$44.50	$445.00
7	Misc	$99.87	$12.33	$343.00	$45.77	$45.00	$45.00	$5.00	$55.00	$665.00	$544.00	$665.00	$33.00
8	Total												

Now we've got a bunch of numbers, but not much else, right? Here's where the fun starts. We're going to tell Excel to total each month's expenses. To do this, we're going to type a formula into cell B8. Click on B8 to make it the active cell. Once you've done that, head to the formula bar beneath the ribbon menu and type the following:

=SUM(B3:B7)

This will tell Excel to add up the cells B3, B4, B5, B6, and B7 and display the total. Once you've entered the formula, press enter. Once you've done that, cell B8 will display something like this:

B8   fx   =SUM(B3:B7)

	A	B	C	D	E	F	G	H	I	J	K	L	M
1	Monthly Expenses												
2		Jan	Feb	Mar	Apr	May	Jun	Jul	Aug	Sep	Oct	Nov	Dec
3	Paper	$11.00	$12.40	$14.78	$99.00	$0.00	$123.40	$33.00	$346.88	$0.00	$33.00	$35.00	$35.88
4	Postage	$14.32	$34.66	$666.00	$645.00	$44.00	$4,444.00	$45.55	$3,556.00	$12.00	$14.56	$333.88	$345.30
5	Envelopes	$12.33	$12.33	$34.00	$12.33	$12.33	$12.33	$12.33	$12.33	$12.33	$12.33	$12.33	$12.33
6	Boxes	$144.33	$12.33	$344.00	$44.00	$445.60	$66.66	$67.77	$565.33	$45.00	$555.40	$44.50	$445.00
7	Misc	$99.87	$12.33	$343.00	$45.77	$45.00	$45.00	$5.00	$55.00	$665.00	$544.00	$665.00	$33.00
8	Total	$281.85											

Now, you *could* spend a bunch of time entering similar formulas in the other rows (C8, D8, etc.), but you've got better things to do, right? Using the flash fill technique we discussed earlier, we can just tell Excel to do the same thing with every other column. Just find the fill button, click it, and drag it to cell M8. Once you've done that, you'll have totals for every month, which will look something like this:

J11   fx

	A	B	C	D	E	F	G	H	I	J	K	L	M
1	Monthly Expenses												
2		Jan	Feb	Mar	Apr	May	Jun	Jul	Aug	Sep	Oct	Nov	Dec
3	Paper	$11.00	$12.40	$14.78	$99.00	$0.00	$123.40	$33.00	$346.88	$0.00	$33.00	$35.00	$35.88
4	Postage	$14.32	$34.66	$666.00	$645.00	$44.00	$4,444.00	$45.55	$3,556.00	$12.00	$14.56	$333.88	$345.30
5	Envelopes	$12.33	$12.33	$34.00	$12.33	$12.33	$12.33	$12.33	$12.33	$12.33	$12.33	$12.33	$12.33
6	Boxes	$144.33	$12.33	$344.00	$44.00	$445.60	$66.66	$67.77	$565.33	$45.00	$555.40	$44.50	$445.00
7	Misc	$99.87	$12.33	$343.00	$45.77	$45.00	$45.00	$5.00	$55.00	$665.00	$544.00	$665.00	$33.00
8	Total	$281.85	$84.05	$1,401.78	$846.10	$546.93	$4,691.39	$163.65	$4,535.54	$734.33	$1,159.29	$1,090.71	$871.51

There you have it. You've created your first spreadsheet. While it's a little on the simple side, everything else you're likely to do with Excel 2013 RT will include the same basic principles, no matter the data you're working with.

*This guide, by its very nature, exists to teach you the basics of Excel spreadsheets. To do some

of the more complex things that are beyond the scope of this guide, you'll have to learn some
formulas that we just don't have space to show you. Head to www.office.com and enter 'Excel
Formulas' in the search bar for an exhaustive list of Excel 2013 formulas.

Let's dig a little deeper now, and discuss a few of the more advanced things we can do with the
worksheet we've just created, shall we?

Working Through Your Worksheet

We've created our sample worksheet and filled it with some data. We've formatted our cells to display dollar amounts, and we've learned how to total our columns. That wasn't so hard, was it? Let's build on all this knowledge and use the very same worksheet to discuss a few of the more advanced things we can do with Excel.

Working with the data we've already got, there are some other numbers we can extrapolate, to help us get an even better idea of our expenses. Let's look at two things: the total money spent on each item, and the average money spent per month on each item. Are you with me so far? Good.

We're going to create another spreadsheet within the same worksheet. Go ahead and select cell E11 and type the words "Average Monthly Expenses". Once you've done that, click on A3 and then hold down the shift key. Next, click cell A8. You've just highlighted all of the expense items in the worksheet:

1	Monthly Expenses	
2		Jan
3	Paper	$
4	Postage	$
5	Envelopes	$
6	Boxes	$1
7	Misc	$
8	Total	$2
9		
10		

Once you've done that, right click and select the menu item labeled 'copy'. Now you've copied those items into the clipboard. Click on cell E13, then right click and select the menu item labeled 'paste'. Now you'll have another little spreadsheet that looks like this:

Average Monthly Expenses
Paper
Postage
Envelopes
Boxes
Misc
Total

Now, just like before, we've got to tell Excel what to do. Luckily, this time, all of our data is already present, we've just got to insert a formula to get the information we want. In this case, we want to display an average of each row, from January through December, in this new column. To do that, we'll insert the formula into cell F13, right next to the word 'paper.' The formula for an average is written in a similar way to the formula for a sum, and it'll look like this:

=AVERAGE(B3:M3)

We're looking to get the average of every row in the paper column of our first spreadsheet. Once you've typed that into cell F13, you'll be presented with something that looks like this:

Average Monthly Expenses	
Paper	$62.03
Postage	
Envelopes	
Boxes	
Misc	
Total	

Now, we *could* apply the formula for the remaining product boxes, but that'd be foolish when we have flash fill at our disposal. Just find the fill button, click, and drag it down to the Misc. label to get averages for every item:

Average Monthly Expenses	
Paper	$62.03
Postage	$846.27
Envelopes	$14.14
Boxes	$231.66
Misc	$213.16
Total	

Click on any of those newly full-of-data cells, and take a look at the formula bar up top. Notice how Excel automatically changed the cells in the formula? Pretty neat.

Now, with our first spreadsheet, we created a total of everything we spent per month. Excel remembers this too, so coming up with a total average of all monthly expenses is as simple as dragging that fill button down one more row to 'total', no new formula necessary!

Average Monthly Expenses	
Paper	$62.03
Postage	$846.27
Envelopes	$14.14
Boxes	$231.66
Misc	$213.16
Total	$1,367.26

To sum up what we've learned with our data, we now know how much we spent, on average, on paper, postage, envelopes, boxes, and miscellaneous items. We *also* now know how much we spent, on average, every month for *all* of this stuff combined. While the data we're using is obviously just an example, you can clearly see how averaging things in this way can really help you to understand things like your own monthly expenses or even how much you spend on specific things like groceries or prescriptions.

There's still more information to be gleaned from that original data, though. When we initially created our spreadsheet, we neglected to ask Excel for the total amount we spent on each individual item. We also don't know how much we've spent this year for everything together, do we? No problem. We've got the data, we just need to tell Excel where to put it.

Go ahead and click on cell I11 and type 'Total Yearly Expenses'. Now click on cell I13 and paste the same items that we just pasted (Paper, Postage, Etc.) into the appropriate places:

	A	B	C	D	E	F	G	H	I	J	K	L	M
1	Monthly Expenses												
2		Jan	Feb	Mar	Apr	May	Jun	Jul	Aug	Sep	Oct	Nov	Dec
3	Paper	$11.00	$12.40	$14.78	$99.00	$0.00	$123.40	$33.00	$346.88	$0.00	$33.00	$35.00	$35.88
4	Postage	$14.32	$34.66	$666.00	$645.00	$44.00	$4,444.00	$45.55	$3,556.00	$12.00	$14.56	$333.88	$345.30
5	Envelopes	$12.33	$12.33	$34.00	$12.33	$12.33	$12.33	$12.33	$12.33	$12.33	$12.33	$12.33	$12.33
6	Boxes	$144.33	$12.33	$344.00	$44.00	$445.60	$66.66	$67.77	$565.33	$45.00	$555.40	$44.50	$445.00
7	Misc	$99.87	$12.33	$343.00	$45.77	$45.00	$45.00	$5.00	$55.00	$665.00	$544.00	$665.00	$33.00
8	Total	$281.85	$84.05	$1,401.78	$846.10	$546.93	$4,691.39	$163.65	$4,535.54	$734.33	$1,159.29	$1,090.71	$871.51
9													
10													
11						Average Monthly Expenses			Total Yearly Expenses				
12													
13						Paper	$62.03		Paper				
14						Postage	$846.27		Postage				
15						Envelopes	$14.14		Envelopes				
16						Boxes	$231.66		Boxes				
17						Misc	$213.16		Misc				
18						Total	$1,367.26		Total				
19													
20													
21													
22													

Now, we know we need to get a sum, not an average, so we'll definitely be using =SUM, but what exactly are we looking for? Well, we want to add everything from B3 to M3 together, right? So the formula we'll enter in cell J13 should be:

=SUM(B3:M3)

Once we've entered that formula into J13, we'll be presented with this:

Total Yearly Expenses	
Paper	$744.34
Postage	
Envelopes	
Boxes	
Misc	
Total	

Now, just like before, let's use that handy fill button to automatically insert the rest of the data, shall we? Once you've done that, you'll be presented with something like this:

Total Yearly Expenses	
Paper	$744.34
Postage	########
Envelopes	$169.63
Boxes	$2,779.92
Misc	$2,557.97
Total	########

Uh oh. What happened? Notice that a couple of our cells are filled with #######. Well, we haven't made an error. Excel simply ran out of room to display those totals, which are more than $9,999.99. Click on any of the cells with ####### and you'll notice that the true number will display as a pop up:

Total Yearly Expenses	
Paper	$744.34
Postage	########
Envelopes	$169.63
Boxes	$2,779.92
Misc	$2,557.97
Total	########
	$16,407.13

Well, the data is there. That's a relief. But how do we get it to show up on our spreadsheet? It's easy: we've just got to make some room by resizing the column.

To resize a column, head to the top of your spreadsheet and find the column you'd like to change. In this case, that will be column J. place the cursor in the bottom right hand corner of the column label, click and the drag it to the right until you see the number appear.

I	J	K
Aug	Sep	Oct
$346.88	$0.00	$:
$3,556.00	$12.00	$1
$12.33	$12.33	$1
$565.33	$45.00	$5!
$55.00	$665.00	$5<
$4,535.54	$734.33	$1,1!

Total Yearly Expenses	
Paper	$744.34
Postage	$10,155.27
Envelope:	$169.63
Boxes	$2,779.92
Misc	$2,557.97
Total	$16,407.13

That's all there is to it.

Now, there's still a lot more data we can tease out of this spreadsheet, namely percentages. We have the data, so let's quickly go over a couple ways to get more information from it. First up: let's find out when we spent the most by figuring out our monthly expenses as a percentage of the whole. To do this, click on cell K21 and type 'Monthly Budget Percentages' and then press enter. In Cell K23, type 'Jan', and then use the fill button to drag down the column to K33, which will be December. Once you've done that, you'll have something that looks like this:

Monthly Budget Percentages	
Jan	
Feb	
Mar	
Apr	
May	
Jun	
Jul	
Aug	
Sep	
Oct	
Nov	
Dec	

Now, we need to figure out percentages for each month. All we need to do is divide our monthly totals (B8, C8, D8, etc.) by our yearly total (J18) and then convert the resulting numbers into a percentage so it's easier to understand. To do this, head to cell L23 and type the following:

=B8/J18

Now, since our data is getting a little bit more complicated, we won't be able to flash fill right away. If we try, Excel will likely not understand what we're trying to do. If this is the case, you'll see error messages that look like this:

Monthly Budget Percentages	
Jan	0.017179
Feb	#DIV/0!
Mar	#DIV/0!
Apr	#DIV/0!
May	#DIV/0!
Jun	#DIV/0!
Jul	#DIV/0!
Aug	#DIV/0!
Sep	#DIV/0!
Oct	#DIV/0!
Nov	#DIV/0!
Dec	#DIV/0!

Go ahead and click on one of these error messages, and look in the formula bar. In our case, instead of the Feb column having the formula =C8/J18, it's got this:

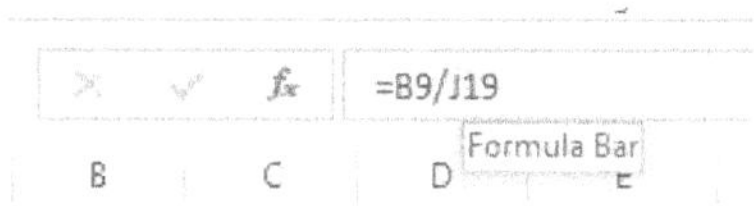

$\times$	$\checkmark$	f_x	=B9/J19	
B		C	D	Formula Bar
				E

Excel is adding a number each time, instead of keeping the second number static. Since there is no data in J19, or J20, and so on, we're left with an error message. No worries, we can just add a couple more formulas manually, and then Excel will begin to understand. First, delete the errors by clicking on cell L24, and then holding shift and clicking L34. Once you've done that, just press the delete key to remove everything within those cells.

Next, Type the formulas for February and March in their respective places:

=D8/J18 and then

=E8/J18

Once you've done that, Excel should have enough information to allow you to fill out the rest of the spreadsheet using the fill button. Once that'd done, you'll have a spreadsheet that looks like this:

Monthly Budget Percentages	
Jan	0.017179
Feb	0.005123
Mar	0.085437
Apr	0.051569
May	0.033335
Jun	0.285936
Jul	0.009974
Aug	0.276437
Sep	0.044757
Oct	0.070658
Nov	0.066478
Dec	0.053118

Now, the data is there and correct, but it looks a little bit confusing. Since we don't really need 6 decimal places of accuracy here, let's go ahead and reformat these cells to percentages so that they're a little easier on the eyes. We have two ways of doing this, both of which start with highlighting the relevant cells (L23 to L24). Once you've highlighted the cells you can right click and then click the menu item labeled 'format cells', and then click 'percentages' and 'ok' on the pop-up menu.

You can also highlight the cells, and then find the format drop-down on the home tab of the ribbon menu. Click it and you'll be presented with this:

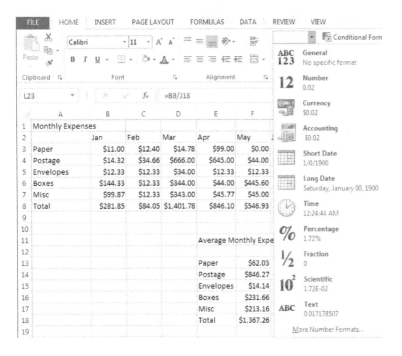

Find the menu item labeled 'percentage' and click it. Whichever method you choose, your spreadsheet will now look like this:

Monthly Budget Percentages

Jan	1.72%
Feb	0.51%
Mar	8.54%
Apr	5.16%
May	3.33%
Jun	28.59%
Jul	1.00%
Aug	27.64%
Sep	4.48%
Oct	7.07%
Nov	6.65%
Dec	5.31%

Now we've got a pretty easy-to-read breakdown of our expenses. We can clearly see, in our example, that we spent the most money in June, and the least money in February. In fact, the months of June and August alone make up over half our yearly expenses. Those two months are way higher than the average, aren't they? But how much higher? We've got the data, so let's find out.

Now, we've already got the average monthly expense on our spreadsheet in cell F18. We also have the total monthly expenses for June and August in cells G8 and I8. So, all we really need to do is divide our monthly totals for those months by the average monthly total, right? To put it in Excel-friendly terms, we enter the formula

=G8/J18 for June

=I8/J18 for August

Which will give us a little spreadsheet that looks like this:

Most Expensive Months

Jun	3.431233
Aug	3.317246

Even though those numbers are greater than 100%, we can still turn them into percentages to get a better idea of what the numbers mean:

Most Expensive Months

Jun	343.12%	More Than Average
Aug	331.72%	More Than Average

That's all there is to it.

Now that we've gone over a lot of things you can do to expand and tease out the data in your worksheets, let's dig a little deeper and begin learning how to make changes to your worksheets.

Ready? Let's go!

Part Three: Getting More out of Excel 2013 RT

Modifying and Refining Your Worksheet

Since we've already got a pretty effective example going, let's continue using our original spreadsheet for this next tutorial. We've got a lot of information about paper, postage, envelopes, and everything else, but what happens when we realize that we've entered some inaccurate data? Let's take a look.

Monthly Expenses

	Jan	Feb	Mar	Apr	May	Jun	Jul	Aug	Sep	Oct	Nov	Dec
Paper	$11.00	$12.40	$14.78	$99.00	$0.00	$123.40	$33.00	$346.88	$0.00	$33.00	$35.00	$35.88
Postage	$14.32	$34.66	$666.00	$645.00	$44.00	$4,444.00	$45.55	$3,556.00	$12.00	$14.56	$333.88	$345.30
Envelopes	$12.33	$12.33	$34.00	$12.33	$12.33	$12.33	$12.33	$12.33	$12.33	$12.33	$12.33	$12.33
Boxes	$144.33	$12.33	$344.00	$44.00	$445.60	$66.66	$67.77	$565.33	$45.00	$555.40	$44.50	$445.00
Misc	$99.87	$12.33	$343.00	$45.77	$45.00	$45.00	$5.00	$55.00	$665.00	$544.00	$665.00	$33.00
Total	$281.85	$84.05	$1,401.78	$846.10	$546.93	$4,691.39	$163.65	$4,535.54	$734.33	$1,159.29	$1,090.71	$871.51

Average Monthly Expenses

Paper	$62.03
Postage	$846.27
Envelopes	$14.14
Boxes	$231.66
Misc	$213.16
Total	$1,367.26

Total Yearly Expenses

Paper	$744.34
Postage	$10,155.27
Envelopes	$169.63
Boxes	$2,779.92
Misc	$2,557.97
Total	$16,407.13

Percentage of Budget

Paper	4.54%
Postage	61.90%
Envelopes	1.03%
Boxes	16.94%
Misc	15.59%
Total	100%

Most Expensive Months

Jun	343.12%	More Than Average
Aug	331.72%	More Than Average

Monthly Budget Percentages

Jan	1.72%
Feb	0.51%
Mar	8.54%
Apr	5.16%
May	3.33%
Jun	28.59%
Jul	1.00%
Aug	27.64%
Sep	4.48%
Oct	7.07%
Nov	6.65%
Dec	5.31%

This worksheet represents everything we've done so far, all the calculations, all the different spreadsheets we've created to deal with the data. All of the numbers below our original spreadsheet are dependent on the numbers above, right? If there's a mistake, you might think that all this data is wasted. Not so. We can modify any of our original data and the changes will be calculated automatically and applied to everything else. As an example, let's take one of our higher expenses and lower it significantly: postage from June (cell G4). To replace this figure with the new, corrected information, just click to activate the cell and enter the new number:

$0.00	$123.40	$33.00
$44.00	44.44	$45.55
$12.33	$12.33	$12.33
$445.60	$66.66	$67.77
$45.00	$45.00	$5.00

Once you hit enter (or an arrow key), the new number is entered. Did you notice anything? Every other relevant number changed to reflect that new number. First, Cell G8 now displays a new total, as the monthly expenses for June have changed. Below that, the Average Monthly Expenses spreadsheet has changed in two ways: the average postage cost, and the average total cost. Ditto with the total yearly expenses to the right of that. Below that, every number in the 'Percentage of Budget' spreadsheet has changed, because every number now represents a different piece of the whole. Make sense? Compare the illustration above to the one below to get a better idea of what's changed.

Monthly Expenses

	Jan	Feb	Mar	Apr	May	Jun	Jul	Aug	Sep	Oct	Nov	Dec
Paper	$11.00	$12.40	$14.78	$99.00	$0.00	$123.40	$33.00	$346.88	$0.00	$33.00	$35.00	$35.88
Postage	$14.32	$34.66	$666.00	$645.00	$44.00	$44.44	$45.55	$3,556.00	$12.00	$14.56	$333.88	$345.30
Envelopes	$12.33	$12.33	$34.00	$12.33	$12.33	$12.33	$12.33	$12.33	$12.33	$12.33	$12.33	$12.33
Boxes	$144.33	$12.33	$344.00	$44.00	$445.60	$66.66	$67.77	$565.33	$45.00	$555.40	$44.50	$445.00
Misc	$99.87	$12.33	$343.00	$45.77	$45.00	$45.00	$5.00	$55.00	$665.00	$544.00	$665.00	$33.00
Total	$281.85	$84.05	$1,401.78	$846.10	$546.93	$291.83	$163.65	$4,535.54	$734.33	$1,159.29	$1,090.71	$871.51

Average Monthly Expenses			Total Yearly Expenses	
Paper	$62.03		Paper	$744.34
Postage	$479.64		Postage	$5,755.71
Envelopes	$14.14		Envelopes	$169.63
Boxes	$231.66		Boxes	$2,779.92
Misc	$213.16		Misc	$2,557.97
Total	$1,000.63		Total	$12,007.57

Percentage of Budget			Monthly Budget Percentages	
Paper	6.20%			
Postage	47.93%		Jan	2.35%
Envelopes	1.41%		Feb	0.70%
Boxes	23.15%		Mar	11.67%
Misc	21.30%		Apr	7.05%
Total	100%		May	4.55%
			Jun	2.43%
			Jul	1.36%
Most Expensive Months			Aug	37.77%
			Sep	6.12%
Jun	29.16%	More Than Average	Oct	9.65%
Aug	453.27%	More Than Average	Nov	9.08%
			Dec	7.26%

By changing just that one number, we've altered the entire spreadsheet. Excel does its part by keeping the math correct. By changing just that one number, we've now stumbled on Excel's main advantage over a piece of paper: it's dynamic. All of the numbers that depend on other numbers will change to reflect any changes you've made. Pretty amazing, isn't it?

Now, changing just that one number has actually negatively affected one of our mini spreadsheets. The 'Most Expensive Months' information that we found relevant in the last section no longer seems so impressive. June is now only 29.16% more expensive than our average month. If we look to the right at the 'Monthly Budget Percentages', we can see that June has now been replaced by August as the most expensive month, while March is now the second most expensive month for our budget. Let's quickly modify that spreadsheet to reflect our new reality.

To change our 'Most Expensive Months' spreadsheet, we'll have to change both the text label and the formula that our number is derived from. First, let's click on 'Jun' and replace it with 'Mar'. You'll then have a spreadsheet that looks like this:

Most Expensive Months		
Mar	29.16%	More Than Average
Aug	453.27%	More Than Average

As you can see, the data hasn't changed, and it still refers to our June numbers. We'll have to enter the formula manually. To do this, click on the cell to activate it, and then take a look at the formula in the formula bar:

=G8/F18

Now, only one piece of this formula really needs to change. The total budget is still located in cell F18, but cell G8 refers to June, not May. Let's correct that by changing G8 to D8, which is the total for March.

Most Expensive Months		
Mar	140.09%	More Than Average
Aug	453.27%	More Than Average

That's all there is to it.

Now, there are some other ways to modify our data without creating a new mini spreadsheet. Let's say that you'd like to change our original spreadsheet into a running total of how much you've spent so far at the end of every month. That sounds like a complex calculation, doesn't it? You're really just a click away. To add different kinds of data to your spreadsheet, just highlight to select all of the data, making sure to leave out the total. Once you've done this, you'll be presented with something that looks like this:

Monthly Expenses												
	Jan	Feb	Mar	Apr	May	Jun	Jul	Aug	Sep	Oct	Nov	Dec
Paper	$11.00	$12.40	$14.78	$99.00	$0.00	$123.40	$33.00	$346.88	$0.00	$33.00	$35.00	$35.88
Postage	$14.32	$34.66	$666.00	$645.00	$44.00	$44.44	$45.55	$3,556.00	$12.00	$14.56	$333.88	$345.30
Envelopes	$12.33	$12.33	$34.00	$12.33	$12.33	$12.33	$12.33	$12.33	$12.33	$12.33	$12.33	$12.33
Boxes	$144.33	$12.33	$344.00	$44.00	$445.60	$66.66	$67.77	$565.33	$45.00	$555.40	$44.50	$445.00
Misc	$99.87	$12.33	$343.00	$45.77	$45.00	$45.00	$5.00	$55.00	$665.00	$544.00	$665.00	$33.00
Total	$281.85	$84.05	$1,401.78	$846.10	$546.93	$291.83	$163.65	$4,535.54		$734.33	$1,159.29	$1,090.71	$871.51

Notice the icon on the bottom right of the selection? Click it to open up a pop-up menu with all sorts of options:

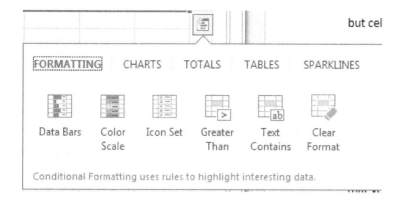

but cel

We'll go over the rest of the options here a little later, but for now, click on the menu item labeled 'Totals'. As you can see, you're given several options for totaling the data in a new way. Excel can perform all of these calculations automatically, based on the selection. To place a running total within your spreadsheet, just click 'Running Total' from the options, and then click 'OK'. Once you've done that, you'll get a confirmation notice that data is already calculated in a different way. Click OK and your spreadsheet will have an entirely different total:

	A	B	C	D	E	F	G	H	I	J	K	L	M
1	Monthly Expenses												
2		Jan	Feb	Mar	Apr	May	Jun	Jul	Aug	Sep	Oct	Nov	Dec
3	Paper	$11.00	$12.40	$14.78	$99.00	$0.00	$123.40	$33.00	$346.88	$0.00	$33.00	$35.00	$35.88
4	Postage	$14.32	$34.66	$666.00	$645.00	$44.00	$44.44	$45.55	$3,556.00	$12.00	$14.56	$333.88	$345.30
5	Envelopes	$12.33	$12.33	$34.00	$12.33	$12.33	$12.33	$12.33	$12.33	$12.33	$12.33	$12.33	$12.33
6	Boxes	$144.33	$12.33	$344.00	$44.00	$445.60	$66.66	$67.77	$565.33	$45.00	$555.40	$44.50	$445.00
7	Misc	$99.87	$12.33	$343.00	$45.77	$45.00	$45.00	$5.00	$55.00	$665.00	$544.00	$665.00	$33.00
8	Running Total	$281.85	$365.90	$1,767.68	$2,613.78	$3,160.71	$3,452.54	$3,616.19	$8,151.73	$8,886.06	$10,045.35	$11,136.06	$12,007.57

As you can see, changing the data is often just that simple. Feel free to experiment with different things within the 'Totals' menu. Remember, you can always undo what you've done using the undo button on the quick access toolbar.

That's all there is to it.

A Quick Note about Templates

Earlier in this guide, we created a new blank worksheet, which we've been working in ever since. We've made a few interesting and useful spreadsheets and populated them with data using our own formulas, creating a good knowledge base for all of our future spreadsheet creations.

So far, we've bypassed working with templates, preferring instead to teach you the basics. It should be noted, however, that the vast majority of things you'll want to do with Excel 2013 RT can be done by slightly modifying existing templates. There are literally thousands of pre-formatted blank workbooks available, covering just about every aspect of Excel.

To get started with templates, click the 'File' menu item from the ribbon menu to open backstage view. From there, click 'New'. You'll be presented with a screen that looks like this:

Clicking any of the pictured templates will show you a larger preview of it, along with some information about what you can do with it. Once you've found one you like, double click it to open it and begin working with it. For this example, we're going to use the 'Simple To-Do List' template.

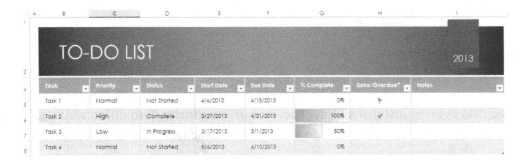

As you can see, things have already been laid out in a pretty beautiful way for you. All you need to do is replace the dummy information with information of your own:

While we always recommend learning as much as you can about any program, the templates that you can find using the search function will probably make up a big percentage of the things you do with Excel 2013 RT.

Beautifying Your Worksheets

Now that we've figured out how to build our own simple worksheets, the time has come to begin crafting the raw data into something a little more pleasing to the eye. Using the example worksheet we've been using over the course of this guide, let's first find a way to make our data pop, and then learn a little about charts and graphs.

To get started with beautifying our spreadsheet, let's deal with our original spreadsheet first. It's full of useful data, but it is a wee bit boring, isn't it? No problem. We can create a table out of it in a couple of simple steps. To do this, highlight the entire spreadsheet, from A1 to M7:

	A	B	C	D	E	F	G	H	I	J	K	L	M
		Jan	Feb	Mar	Apr	May	Jun	Jul	Aug	Sep	Oct	Nov	Dec
1	Monthly Expenses												
2	Paper	$11.00	$12.40	$14.78	$99.00	$0.00	$123.40	$33.00	$346.88	$0.00	$33.00	$35.00	$35.88
3	Postage	$14.32	$34.66	$666.00	$645.00	$44.00	$44.00	$45.55	$3,556.00	$12.00	$14.56	$333.88	$345.30
4	Envelopes	$12.33	$12.33	$34.00	$12.33	$12.33	$4,444.00	$12.33	$12.33	$12.33	$12.33	$12.33	$12.33
5	Boxes	$144.33	$12.33	$344.00	$44.00	$445.60	$66.66	$67.77	$565.33	$45.00	$555.40	$44.50	$445.00
6	Misc	$99.87	$12.33	$343.00	$45.77	$45.00	$45.00	$5.00	$55.00	$665.00	$544.00	$665.00	$33.00
7	Total	$281.85	$84.05	$1,401.78	$846.10	$546.93	$4,723.06	$163.65	$4,535.54	$734.33	$1,159.29	$1,090.71	$871.51
8													
9													

Once you've done that, head to the ribbon menu and find the menu item labeled 'Format as Table'. Clicking there will bring up a colorful list of potential tables we can use. Notice that they look a little bit like the To-Do list from the templates section? Find a color/design you like and then click on it. Once you've done that, our spreadsheet will magically turn into something resembling this:

	A	B	C	D	E	F	G	H	I	J	K	L	M
1	Monthly Expenses ▾	Jan ▾	Feb ▾	Mar ▾	Apr ▾	May ▾	Jun ▾	Jul ▾	Aug ▾	Sep ▾	Oct ▾	Nov ▾	Dec ▾
2	Paper	$11.00	$12.40	$14.78	$99.00	$0.00	$123.40	$33.00	$346.88	$0.00	$33.00	$35.00	$35.88
3	Postage	$14.32	$34.66	$666.00	$645.00	$44.00	$44.00	$45.55	$3,556.00	$12.00	$14.56	$333.88	$345.30
4	Envelopes	$12.33	$12.33	$34.00	$12.33	$12.33	$4,444.00	$12.33	$12.33	$12.33	$12.33	$12.33	$12.33
5	Boxes	$144.33	$12.33	$344.00	$44.00	$445.60	$66.66	$67.77	$565.33	$45.00	$555.40	$44.50	$445.00
6	Misc	$99.87	$12.33	$343.00	$45.77	$45.00	$45.00	$5.00	$55.00	$665.00	$544.00	$665.00	$33.00
7	Total	$281.85	$84.05	$1,401.78	$846.10	$546.93	$4,723.06	$163.65	$4,535.54	$734.33	$1,159.29	$1,090.71	$871.51
8													

Not bad. Of course, we don't *have* to make a table out of everything. We can color our cells, rows, and columns in any way we like. This method is particularly handy when working with smaller amounts of data, like our mini-spreadsheets. To manually color a spreadsheet, simply highlight the cell, column, or row, and then right click. Once you've done that, you'll be greeted with the context menu:

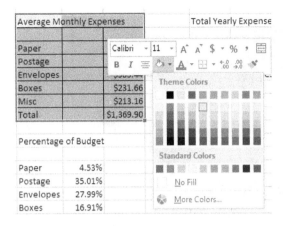

Average Monthly Expenses		Total Yearly Expense
Paper		
Postage		
Envelopes		
Boxes	$231.66	
Misc	$213.16	
Total	$1,369.90	

Percentage of Budget	
Paper	4.53%
Postage	35.01%
Envelopes	27.99%
Boxes	16.91%

From here, you can change the color of any cell, or range of cells. It's important to note, however, that subtlety goes a long way when it comes to coloring your spreadsheets.

Now that we've made our spreadsheets look a little nicer, let's take a minute to discuss charts and graphs. Excel 2013 RT has some quick ways to create really beautiful illustrations of your data. All you need to do to get started is highlight one of your spreadsheets. For this example, we're going to create a chart that will show us visually where our money is going.

To get started, let's highlight the 'Percentage of Budget' spreadsheet. Once you've done that, click the button on the bottom right hand corner of the device to bring up the formatting pop-up:

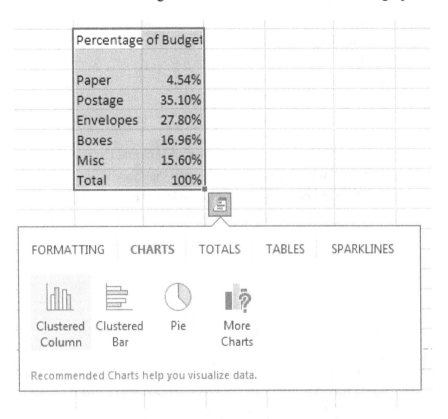

Click on the 'Charts' menu item, and then choose from any of the four options. In our example, we chose 'Clustered Column' and were presented with a chart that looks like this:

As you can see, the only modification we made was adding a title by clicking in the title box. The rest of the data comes from the spreadsheet. Once a chart is made it can be repositioned, resized, and moved wherever you like on the worksheet space.

These charts and graphs don't actually take up any cells on your spreadsheet, but are actually placed *on top* of the cells, so you can move them wherever you like without affecting the data on your worksheet.

That's all there is to it.

> *Feel free to experiment with any of the various kinds of charts and graphs. Keep in mind that all the graphs and charts you make in this way are dynamic, meaning that as long as you're using the data from your worksheet, the numbers will always be right, and the graphs will actually change if the data in your spreadsheet is changed (just like we discussed in the 'Modifying and Refining Your Worksheet' section of this guide.)*

Saving and Sharing Your Worksheets

Now that we've created a few spreadsheets, input some data, learned a few formulas, and made some beautiful charts, the time has come to finalize our document and send it out into the world. The first thing you'll want to do when you've finished a document is save it. This can be done easily enough by click (or tapping on) the File tab on the ribbon menu, which will take you to the backstage view. From here, click 'Save As' to save your document, which will open the Save As view:

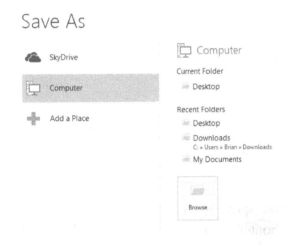

As you can see, you have a couple of options. You can either save the workbook to your Windows RT tablet by clicking 'Computer' or save it to SkyDrive. Saving your work to SkyDrive will give us more sharing options, which we'll go over in a minute. In either case, just browse for the folder you'd like to save your workbook in and click it, then click Save. That's all there is to it.

Once you've saved your work, you can begin the process of protecting it. While this doesn't come up very often in other Office programs, Excel utilizes all of those formulas and cell references that we've been dealing with throughout this guide, and (as you know) changing the wrong number can screw up the entirety of your workbook. This is why it's important to protect your Excel RT 2013 documents. To get started, click the 'Info' tab in backstage view. You'll be presented with a menu on the right, the first item of which is labeled 'Protect Workbook'. The easiest way to protect your project is to use the first menu item 'Mark as final', which will turn your workbook 'Read-Only' for anyone else who opens it.

Info

Now that we've saved and protected our document, we can share it with the world. You might not always want to do this, but it can come in handy for certain kinds of spreadsheets – namely work or hobby-related files. There are a couple of ways to go about sharing. To get started, head to the backstage area and find the menu item labeled 'Share'. Once you've clicked on it, you'll be greeted with this menu:

If your document is saved to SkyDrive (we hope it is!), you'll have a few options here. On the right, you can type the names and/or email addresses of people you'd like to invite to view the document. If you'd rather just give out a link to people on your own, click 'Get a Sharing Link' and copy the URL, sending it to whoever you like. If you'd like to share it with Facebook or Twitter, tap 'Post to Social Networks' and follow the prompts.

The final way to share your document is by emailing it. Clicking here will actually bring up a list of email options. This requires a little bit of explanation.

Share

Example
Brian Flanagan's SkyDrive

Share

👥 Invite People

🔗 Get a Sharing Link

👥 Post to Social Networks

✉ Email

Email

📧 Send as Attachment
▪ Everyone gets a copy to review

💻 Send a Link
▪ Everyone works on the same copy of this workbook
▪ Everyone sees the latest changes
▪ Keeps the email size small

📄 Send as PDF
▪ Everyone gets a PDF attachment
▪ Preserves layout, formatting, fonts, and images
▪ Content can't be easily changed

📄 Send as XPS
▪ Everyone gets an XPS attachment
▪ Preserves layout, formatting, fonts, and images
▪ Content can't be easily changed

📠 Send as Internet Fax
▪ No fax machine needed
▪ You'll need a fax service provider

As we mentioned at the beginning of this guide, your Excel 2013 RT documents will be saved in the .xlsx format. What this means, practically speaking, is that people running older versions of Excel might not be able to read your documents correctly, and people not using Excel at all might not be able to read them at all. That's why Microsoft has given you so many options in this section. You can email an attachment in PDF (Adobe's Portable Document Format) to make sure that everyone sees your spreadsheets as you intended them to, which can really come in handy. It's a good idea to ask prospective recipients what format they'd prefer before sending them out.

Conclusion

Well, that's about it. You should be well on your way to mastering Excel 2013 RT. You should now be able to navigate your way around, create some interesting spreadsheets, add and remove data, create charts and graphs, and share the result with the world. You can take a project from a blank slate to a finished masterpiece. You can take a template and input your information, making it entirely your own. We've shown you the essentials, but more importantly, we've tried to instill in you the confidence to tackle any kind of spreadsheet task that might come your way tomorrow, while allowing you to get things done today.

We sincerely hope you've enjoyed reading this guide as much as we've enjoyed writing it. We're sure that you'll be getting plenty of use out of Office RT 2013 on your Windows RT tablet for years to come.

Thanks for reading!

About Minute Help Press

Minute Help Press is building a library of books for people with only minutes to spare. Follow @minutehelp on Twitter to receive the latest information about free and paid publications from Minute Help Press, or visit minutehelpguides.com.